Leadership

Three Key Employee-Centered Elements
With Case Studies

by

Marc Summerfield

Summerfield Consulting

Bel Air, Maryland
Marc@SummerfieldConsulting.org

LEADERSHIP

LEADERSHIP

Contents

LEADERSHIP

Introduction

The purpose of this book is to explain the three employee-centered elements of leadership—connection, gratitude, and responsiveness.

In our organizational lives, we yearn for true leadership. We bemoan the impotence of leadership in our social, civic, and religious organizations, in our government, and in our workplaces. Although Kouzes and Posner claim that "love is the soul of leadership," [1] we do not go to work each day seeking love. We seek leadership. We want to fill the leadership void with people who are effective and produce desired effects.

However, this book is not about emotional intelligence (EI). That is the ability to identify, assess, and control the emotions of oneself, of others, and of groups.

Nor is this book about servant leadership. That is a broad management philosophy that implies a comprehensive view of the quality of people, work, and community spirit.

Nor is this book a miniature version of Stephen Covey's *The Seven Habits of Highly Effective People.* Covey presents a complex, research-based framework for personal and professional effectiveness.[2]

So this book does not pretend to challenge the power, structure, or validity of the emotional-intelligence philosophy, the servant-leadership model, or the seven habits. It merely describes three employee-centered elements, which when judiciously and continuously applied, improve a leader's chances of driving meaningful and enduring change.

The three employee-centered elements—connection, gratitude, and responsiveness—appear limited in scope, almost inadequate, but they are deceiving. Each element encompasses a wide range of skills, traits, and qualities. The three elements represent a mnemonic, which when accessed, opens a window into human-relations leadership—a window that might otherwise be closed.

The challenge is to devise an employee-centered triad—three sets of behaviors that don't necessarily compose the complete range of human-relations behaviors but provide a substantial start on the road to success. Such behaviors are not only meaningful in themselves, but they also provide a foundation on which to build. Application of the triad throughout an organization promotes consistency of approach to human relations, shapes the priorities, and fuels cultural uniformity.

The remainder of this document focuses on how leaders can use the triad to work with employees and engage them to drive change.

CHAPTER 1

The Essence and Nature of Leadership

Historian David McCullough's book, *The Great Bridge,* tells the story of the Roebling family in New York City. John Roebling, the Roebling patriarch, was a German-born and German-trained bridge engineer. After a series of pre- and post-Civil War successes, Roebling promoted his design of a bridge to connect lower Manhattan with Brooklyn over the East River—a bridge to fuel the population and economic growth of Brooklyn.[1]

After navigating political and financial obstacles, John Roebling crushed his foot while surveying the site, contracted tetanus, and died soon after. His son, Washington Roebling, grasped the leadership baton and assumed the role of chief engineer to execute his father's design.

Early in the construction, tragedy struck Washington when he contracted caisson disease (the "bends") working at the construction site. Sickly and disabled, Washington retreated to his apartment in Brooklyn Heights, which overlooked the area. Determined not to allow the project to falter, Washington and his wife, Emily, became a storied professional partnership. Emily "stepped in and provided the critical written link between her husband and the engineers."[2] On May 24, 1883, Emily and Washington Roebling witnessed the joyous opening of the Brooklyn Bridge.

The story of the Roeblings exemplifies the shared execution of what we are calling the "change triad"—1) creating a vision; 2) having confidence in the vision and in oneself to execute the vision; 3) and acting on that vision.

John Roebling created the vision of the bridge. He had confidence in the vision and in his ability to execute it, but he was unable to act. Rather, Washington, with confidence in his father's vision and in his own ability to execute it, assumed the leadership role.

And finally, Emily, with confidence in her husband and in her own ability as confidant and conduit, teamed with her husband to act on the vision and convert it into the monumental reality that it remains today. All three Roeblings were leaders.

What Is a Leader or Leadership?

Note the following six definitions of *leaders* or *leadership*:

"Leadership is taking people to places they've never been before."[3] — Marie Kane

"Leadership is the process of influencing the activities of an organization group toward goal achievement."[4] — C. F. Rauch and O. Behling

"The leader is one who mobilizes others toward a goal shared by leaders and followers. Leaders, followers, and goals make up the three equally necessary supports for leadership."[5] — Garry Wills

"Great leaders rally people to a better future."[6] — Marcus Buckingham

"The fundamental purpose of leadership is to produce useful change, especially non-incremental change."[7] — John Kotter

"Leadership is a process whereby an individual influences a group of individuals to achieve a common goal."[8] — Peter Northouse

The definitions above are clear, strong, and meaningful, but Peter Northouse's definition captures the essence of leadership. He infuses an ethical component: the leader influences rather than dictates. Ken Blanchard agrees: "The key to successful leadership today is influence, not authority."[9]

In the second part of his definition, Northouse infuses a participative component: the leader works to achieve a common goal, one jointly agreed upon.

Modern thinking embraces both notions. First, a good leader applies influence throughout the change process, and second, he or she tries to achieve a common goal. Ken Blanchard states, "Leadership is not something you do to people. It's something you do with people."[10]

Therefore, if leaders are enlightened, the process is a joint effort to achieve a common goal. In fact, good leadership is a process that achieves a goal.

Leaders Drive Change

Leaders create change. Jeffrey Immelt, the chief executive officer of General Electric, says, "Great leaders drive change."[11] His statement will serve as our operational definition. Because Immelt's adjective *great* and his verb *drive* add loftiness, passion, and style, the result is more inspiring than the bland alternative, "Leaders create change" or the version offered by Rick Pitino, present head basketball coach of the University of Louisville Cardinals: "Leadership is all about change."[12] John Maxwell agrees with Immelt but turns Immelt's statement upside down. Maxwell states, "No great leader in history has fought to prevent change."[13]

Immelt's definition mirrors Peter Drucker's assertion that "management is doing things right; leadership is doing the right things."[14] Naturally, if the "right things" differ from the current state, then leaders drive change to achieve the right things. Abraham Lincoln drove change from slavery to freedom and from secession to unity. Mohandas Gandhi drove change from occupation to independence. Martin Luther King Jr. drove change from oppression to tolerance.

Although great leaders drive change, great leaders do not drive change recklessly. They manage the purpose and rate of change. Lincoln, Gandhi, and Martin Luther King Jr. were acutely aware of this. Lincoln's goal of the "Emancipation Proclamation" was unquestioned, and his timing was legendary. Gandhi's quest for an independent India was accomplished through patient but persistent nonviolence. But Martin Luther King Jr. bemoaned the lack of progress toward his dream. He cried, "One hundred years later [after the "Emancipation Proclamation"], the Negro is still languishing in the corners of American society and finds himself an exile in his own land."[15]

An appealing characteristic of Immelt's definition is the lowercase *l* in *leaders*. He implies that each of us, even those with titles that do not begin with uppercase letters, such as nurse, shortstop, or school-board member, can drive consequential change. The concept of being a small *l* leader (emergent leadership) as opposed to big *L* (assigned leadership) is empowering. It encourages action despite the absence of an impressive title, high salary, or corner office. Emergent leadership negates the notion that workers, team members, or customers have no responsibility or authority to drive change. Emergent leaders are not indifferent observers or passive participants.

In the leadership game, all can be coaches or managers in addition to being spectators or players.

Celtics coach Rick Pitino says, "Ever since I came to the Boston Celtics in 1997, I have been looking for some players who are going to become leaders. From the great Celtics teams of the eighties with Larry Bird, to the Lakers of the same era, to the Chicago Bulls with Michael Jordan, a common thread running through these teams was the presence of great leadership on the court. Bird, Magic, and Jordan were not just great basketball players. They were great leaders as well—to the point that if teammates did not work hard in practice, *they* would get on them. These great players constantly reinforced the coach's principles and strategies."[16]

Mother Teresa said, "Do not wait for leaders; do it alone, person to person."[17] Comedienne Lily Tomlin offers the same sentiment with a humorous twist: "I always wondered why somebody doesn't do something about that. Then I realized I was somebody."[18] By doing Mother Teresa's *it* or Lily Tomlin's *that*, we become leaders ourselves. Leadership is not the sole domain of a president, chief executive officer, director, or reverend.

There are alternatives to the driving-change theme of leadership. Maybe a "component of the theme" is a better representation. John Kotter claims that leadership is "about coping with change,"[19] professing a need to be adaptive and nimble. Jim Calhoun, coach of the 2011 National Collegiate Athletic Association (NCAA) champion University of Connecticut Husky men's basketball team, claims that "good leaders sell change," conveying the wisdom of inclusion.[20] In fact, leaders probably do all three (*drive, cope, sell*) depending upon the leader's style and circumstances, but "driving change" is preferred because it embodies excitement, which propels us to a better future.

Vision

Great leaders drive change by:
1. Creating a vision
2. Embodying confidence in the vision and in oneself to execute the vision
3. Exemplifying a propensity to act on that vision. Tom Peters refers to this step as a "bias for action."[21]

Warren Bennis supports this mobilizing "change" triad by asserting, "Leadership is the capacity to translate vision into reality. Vision, step 1; capacity, step 2; reality, step 3."[22]

Each step of the change triad encompasses a literature of its own, especially when creating a vision—a mental model of an ideal future state. Some leaders promote vision as the key to organizational change. Theodore Hesburgh agrees: "The very essence of leadership is that you have to have vision."[23] In the leadership sense, vision is usually broad, towering, and transformational, but the change triad works just as well when the vision is a goal or an objective—specific, less ambitious, and incremental.

Some offer an existential approach to vision. Existential thought proclaims, "You have to bear responsibility for making your way through life and creating some kind of meaning for it."[24] Peter Zarlenga proclaims, "To come to be you must have a vision of Being, a Dream, a Purpose, a Principle. You will become what your vision is."[25] Oprah Winfrey expresses the same: "Create the highest, grandest vision possible for your life because you become what you believe."[26] Zarlenga and Winfrey present a vision as a prerequisite for *being* and *becoming.*

Translated to leadership, the leader is compelled to form a vision with and for the organization. The *you* in, "You will become what your vision is," or "You become what you believe" can be your organization.

However, a connection between the vision and the outcome of being is not absolute. Mike Vance and Diane Deacon, proponents of creative thinking, admit that although we are taught to believe that "the human spirit is indomitable and can accomplish virtually anything, logicians will add that we can do nothing outside the realm of truth and reality."[27] Nevertheless, acting with the premise of the connection between the vision and the outcome is more than just constructive. It is empowering and likely predictive, which justifies its prevalence in inspirational literature and speeches. The poet Shel Silverstein casts the message for children.[28]

> *"Listen to the mustn'ts, child. Listen to the don'ts. Listen to the shouldn'ts, the impossibles, the won'ts. Listen to the never haves, then listen close to me. Anything can happen, child. Anything can be."*
>
> — *Shel Silverstein*

As important as vision is, it is only the first step. The domino metaphor is not useful. If vision is the first domino, it is not true that once the first domino falls, the other dominos will fall and change will ensue. Antoine de Saint-Exupery, author of *The Little Prince*, wrote, "A rock pile ceases to be a rock pile the moment a single man contemplates it, bearing within him the image of a cathedral."[29]

Well, not quite. In spite of his inspirational message, visions must grow two legs—confidence and action.

Confidence

According to the dictionary, confidence is a "belief in oneself and one's powers and abilities." Stuart Levine maintains that the foundation for confidence is a person's value system.[30] Confidence in one's own value system produces a confident persona as well as a confidence for making decisions and taking action. Confidence is a commonly listed leadership trait, and, in fact, is one of the four positive psychological capacities of the authentic leadership model—the others being hope, optimism, and resilience. Cicero links confidence to change, and he says, "Confidence is that feeling by which the mind embarks in great and honorable courses with a sure hope and trust in itself."[31]

Step two mandates a confidence in the vision in addition to a confidence in oneself. Jesse Jackson's rhythmical quotation addresses confidence in a vision as "something my heart can believe." He declares, "If my mind can conceive it, and my heart can believe it, I know I can achieve it."[32] President Harry Truman is more pragmatic than Jackson but still hopeful, "Believe and you're halfway there."[33]

Action

Step three depicts an intrinsic, natural tendency to go for it, get it done, and bring it home. Catherine Pulsifer, glass artist and author, says, "The dreams I only thought about, the ones I took no action on, well, they are still dreams. But the ones that I took action on, they are now a reality."[34] Steps one and two are fruitless without step three. In fact, according to Pablo Picasso, "Action is the foundational key to all success."[35]

Below are five quotations that promote the action-oriented approach:

"There comes a moment when you have to stop revving up the car and shove it into gear."[36] — David Mahoney

"What is the purpose of a plan if we do not work it?"[37] — John Wanamaker

"Nothing will ever be attempted if all possible objections must first be overcome."[38] — Samuel Johnson

"All truth passes through three stages. First, it is ridiculed. Second, it is violently opposed. Third, it is accepted as being self-evident."[39] — Arnold Schopenhauer

"A man would do nothing if he waited until he could do it so well that no one could find fault."[40] — Cardinal John Henry Newman

Roslyn Carter, recognizing the adversity and challenges that face the leader who is determined to drive change, combines steps two and three: "You have to have confidence in your ability and then be tough enough to follow through."[41]

The Eight-Stage Process
The adopted three-step change triad omits the process of implementing change, which can be viewed as a management function, but it is more commonly viewed as an amalgamation of leadership and management. Kotter's "eight-stage process" of making ("driving") change depicts this amalgamation:

1. Establishing a sense of urgency
2. Forming a powerful guiding coalition
3. Creating a vision
4. Communicating the vision

5. Empowering others to act on the vision
6. Planning for and creating short-term wins
7. Consolidating improvements and producing still more change
8. Institutionalizing new approaches[42]

Kotter's process is admittedly richer than the three-step approach. Some elements overlap, but his process has eight steps, burdened by the memory and recall challenges associated with eight steps instead of the change triad's three steps.

Although the leader may serve as the visionary, the catalyst, and the champion, an enlightened environment mandates that the followers participate in the change process. Among the variety of leadership theories and approaches, such as the triad approach, the skills approach, style approach, situational approach, contingency theory, leader-member exchange theory, transformational leadership, authentic leadership, team leadership, and the ethical approach (including servant leadership), all enlist employees significantly.

The leadership imperative to involve employees has many origins. One has an ethical base; it is the right thing to do. Actions that promote participation and equity have powerful ethical overtones. Another is pragmatic; employee involvement molds the quality of the outcome. In 2001, Douglas Conant, the newly designated chief executive officer (CEO) of Campbell Soups, noticed that "employee engagement had tanked." He sought to reverse that immediately because of his staunch belief that high performance hinged upon high engagement.[43]

Vance and Deacon suggest, "Involvement is the primary method for inculcating a caring attitude into our characters. When you want to develop the positive attributes of a caring person, such as passion, commitment, tenacity, and dedication, the secret is to get the person or persons involved. It isn't enough to make people feel part of something; they must become part of something."[44] The path from feeling to becoming is evolutionary and can mimic a magical mystery tour. It takes a menagerie of nouns to make the journey: patience, persistence, energy, commitment, and sacrifice. As the child becomes the adult or the larvae becomes the butterfly, the collection of individuals morph into a different entity—an effective team. Employees gel and soar when they are integral to change.

The nature of the leader-follower relationship is a vital component of becoming part of something. One of the most important relationships in the workplace is that of leader and follower. Indira Gandhi ponders, "I suppose that leadership at one time meant muscles; but today it means getting along with people."[45]

The core of the leader-follower relationship is human relations. Katz depicts the human-relations skill set as one of the three personal skill sets that define effective leadership—the other two being technical and conceptual.[46] He contends that conceptual skill dominates technical skill in importance at the top management level and that technical skill dominates conceptual skill at the supervisory level (see figure). But the human-relations pillar is equally important at all three levels of management—supervisory (front line), middle management, and top management.

Skills Needed—Skills Approach			
Top Management		Human	Conceptual
	Technical		
Middle Management	Technical	Human	Conceptual
Supervisory Management	Technical	Human	
			Conceptual

P. Northouse, *Leadership: Theory and Practice.* p. 41. Figure 3.1

A reasonable premise is that technical expertise is a prerequisite for promoting technical/clinical personnel, e.g., engineers, nurses, and construction workers, into leadership roles. In 1969, educator Laurence J. Peter proposed, "In a hierarchy, every employee tends to rise to his level of incompetence."[47] If the "Peter principle" is valid, and if promotions are based significantly on technical competence, then incompetence stems from deficiencies related to nontechnical aspects. Because conceptual skills are less important for the frontline manager, the human-relations skills are pivotal. Technical personnel often lack formal human-relations training when promoted, so all but the most talented often fall short. They either struggle to meet performance standards, retreat to their former positions, or leave the organization, either voluntarily or involuntarily.

The human-relations field is vast. Many leaders desire to be accomplished at human relations, but the practical challenges of immersing themselves into this vastness are daunting. The fact that many hesitate or stall doesn't render their desire disingenuous.

Some organizations provide internal training—well-intended attempts to infuse human-relations skills quickly and increase the likelihood of a successful transition from peer to supervisor. But how is the information best packaged and presented? W. J. King and James Skakoon assert that "the faculty for reducing apparently complicated situations to their basic, essential elements is a form of wisdom. Make it your practice to integrate, condense, summarize, and simplify your facts, rather than expand, ramify, complicate, and disintegrate them."[48]

In this spirit, the reader can explore three popular and enduring summaries of human-relations leadership: Spears,[49] Sipe and Frick's[50] and Li's.[51] Spears outlines ten principles of servant leadership, and Sipe and Frick offer seven pillars of servant leadership, both based on Robert Greenleaf's writings.[52] Li outlines five new rules of open leadership. But the search persists. After applying talent analytics, Google's® Project Oxygen, "so named because good management keeps the company alive," recently devised "eight behaviors that characterize good managers."[53, 54, 55]

Because research shows that memory decreases considerably after three-to-five elements,[56] the challenge is to simplify the human-relations aspect from the ten principles, seven pillars, and five rules to three memorable elements. The power of the triad is intriguing. Although it's not entirely clear why three rather than two or four or more should be the iconic grouping, the ability of humans to register and recall a set of three could be a key reason. Examples include the arts trilogies: (*Godfather; Lord of the Rings*); literature (*The Three Musketeers; Three Blind Mice*); music (The Bee Gees; The Supremes); religion and spirituality (the Father, the Son, the Holy Spirit); popular culture (The Three Stooges); business (AAA®, IBM®, AT&T®); and history and politics ("The Gettysburg Address": "of the people, by the people, for the people") ("The Declaration of Independence": "life, liberty, and the pursuit of happiness").

The challenge is to devise an employee-centered triad—three sets of behaviors that don't necessarily compose the complete range of human-relations behaviors but provide a substantial start on the road to success—behaviors that are meaningful by themselves and also provide a foundation to build upon.

The employee-centered triad's simplicity has liabilities and assets. Admittedly, a loss of completeness occurs. But the simplicity promotes understanding and recall of the elements, so leaders are more apt to apply them. Application of the triad throughout an organization promotes consistency of approach to human relations, shapes the priorities, and fuels cultural uniformity.

Driving Change

There is one more question to answer: Why drive change? Are we driving change solely to become more efficient or more effective, to become more prestigious or more profitable, or to augment programs and services? Does a common mission unify all leaders, regardless of their businesses, jobs, or disciplines, regardless of each organization's vision, mission, and values? Do leaders have a common mission regardless of whether they lead clerks, nurses, or construction workers—regardless of whether their employees fill orders, wipe brows, or insert steel beams? Is there a higher-level, common mission, a sense of purpose that all leaders can recall during moments of adversity and triumph? Does a sense of purpose deeply affect and inspire leaders beyond the meaning and rewards associated with the visions, goals, and objectives?

The Wilson Challenge

Woodrow Wilson, the twenty-eighth president of the United States, provided this sense of purpose. In three short sentences, he made a unifying declaration that challenges us to recognize and pursue a higher-level, common mission.

> "You are not here merely to make a living. You are here in order to enable the world to live more amply, with greater vision, and with a finer spirit of hope and achievement. You are here to enrich the world, and you impoverish yourself if you forget the errand."[57] — Woodrow Wilson

Wilson recognized that most of us work to make a living, but he clearly stated a nobler, broader mission: "to enable the world to live more amply."

Wilson challenges us to define our world. Lincoln's world encompassed slaves and citizens of the United States of America; Gandhi's world involved the British and the East Indians; and Martin Luther King Jr.'s world focused on American blacks and whites. As leaders of organizations, our world need not be as expansive. Our world may comprise board members, colleagues, employees, customers, vendors, clients, members, congregants, students, or our patients.

Then, Wilson completed the circle. After he told us that we are "not here merely to make a living," that we are here "to enable the world to live more amply," he implored us not to "forget the errand" lest we "impoverish" ourselves. He reminded us that our efforts are not entirely altruistic, and that beyond the self-centered benefit of making a living, accepting Wilson's challenge rewards each of us with a profound sense of fulfillment.

Combating Three Signs of a Miserable Job

In 2007, Patrick Lencioni published *The Three Signs of a Miserable Job*. He defines a miserable job as one that "makes a person cynical and frustrated and demoralized when he/she goes home at night."[58] He identifies three signs: anonymity, irrelevance, and immeasurement. According to Lencioni: "*Anonymity* is the feeling that employees get when they realize that their manager has little interest in them."[59] Mother Teresa agreed. "The most terrible poverty is loneliness and the feeling of being unloved."[60]

Lencioni wrote, "*Irrelevance* takes root when employees cannot see how their jobs make a difference in the lives of others."[61] Publisher Katharine Graham voiced the same opinion: "To love what you do and feel it matters—how can anything be more fun?"[62]

Lencioni said, "*Immeasurement* is the inability of employees to assess for themselves their contribution or success."[63] David Novak agreed when he said, "People are moved by what is truly measured."[64]

Each of the three employee-centered elements combats one or more of the three signs of a miserable job.

Traits and Skills

Although traits and skills that enable leadership success are excluded from Jeffrey Immelt's definition that "great leaders drive change," traits and skills occupy a considerable portion of leadership research, thought, and text. Skills are abilities that can be acquired and developed, but traits tend to be innate, "hard-wired" characteristics. Although writing and speaking are skills, and dependability and assertiveness are traits, some scholars contend that talent plays a role in the former and diligence and determination develop the latter.

Authors categorize traits and skills differently. Whereas Gary Yukl[65] and Peter Northouse[66] describe traits and skills as separate entities, Marie Kane[67] and John Gardner[68] combine the traits and skills into one list of attributes. John Maxwell[69] combines the traits and skills into one list of "indispensable qualities." John Zenger, Joseph Folkman, and Scott Edinger list sixteen "leadership competencies" that correlate strongly with positive business outcomes.[70]

Many scholars reject the notion that a specific skill or trait or set of skills or traits is necessary for effective leadership. They emphasize some and de-emphasize others. Not only that, many acknowledge that leadership is situational, that is, traits and skills that contribute to success in one situation might falter in another.[71] The accomplished leader must be agile, applying different sets of traits and skills, depending upon the constituency, the setting, the importance, the sense of urgency, and the goal. In a broader sense, traits and skills that contribute to success in one discipline, business type, or profession might not work in another. Most of the generals who became president were abject failures. Ulysses S. Grant famously stated, "War and politics are so different."[72]

LEADERSHIP

CHAPTER 2

Connection

communication • coordination • coaching • consideration
commitment • collaboration • confrontation • cohesiveness

Connection combats anonymity and irrelevance.

In 1992, an obscure governor from a poor and sparsely populated state navigated the Democratic Party's primaries successfully and was on a trajectory to the presidency. Few citizens and political experts predicted this, except Governor Clinton himself and perhaps, Hillary, his wife.

It appears that Bill Clinton was "driving change" by following the change triad:

- Creating a vision (to be president)
- Having confidence in the vision and in himself to execute the vision
- Acting on that vision

On a fall evening in 1992, Clinton stood on the stage at the University of Richmond in Virginia at the second of three debates with his prime contenders: President George H.W. Bush and businessman Ross Perot.

In one widely publicized exchange, Clinton so outmaneuvered his opponents, especially President Bush, that in the span of several minutes, he catapulted himself into a position to win the election. He did this by connecting with a young lady who had asked a provocative question. While doing so, he was simultaneously connecting with millions of Americans, who then viewed him in an entirely different light. This obscure governor from Arkansas, a state whose commonly known favorite sons included only Brooks Robinson, Johnny Cash, and Glen Campbell, transformed his image from an ambitious, little known, long-winded upstart into an intelligent, charismatic, credible presidential hopeful.

The exchange began with the young lady asking the candidates how the national debt affected them personally. First, President Bush responded. Before answering, he glanced at his watch—an ill-fated move frequently cited as a memorable presidential-debate moment.[1] No one but Bush knew his intent, but many interpreted the gesture as a display of boredom or eagerness for the evening to end. Once Bush began speaking, he struggled to understand the question, appeared impatient and uninterested, and according to Alex Markels, "showed himself to be out of touch with ordinary Americans."[2]

Then, it was Clinton's turn. He briskly walked toward the young lady, closing the physical and psychological distance. After making eye contact, he engaged her instantly by stating, "Tell me how it's affected you. Do you know people who have lost their jobs, lost their homes?" He alertly truncated her response without appearing rude but not allowing her to consume his precious time. Clinton displayed his confidence and humility by unashamedly admitting that he was the governor of a small state. He displayed sensitivity by stating emphatically, "In my state, when people lose their jobs, there is a good chance I know them by their names." He displayed his intelligence and knowledge by demonstrating a razor-sharp understanding of the issues. He displayed his uncanny ability to communicate through his measured and cadenced responses. Clinton did all this in the span of ninety seconds.

When Clinton leapt to his feet, he focused on the young lady and on her alone. He acted as if no one else were in the room and that the cameras were not rolling. This approach encapsulated the two within an invisible tube and connected them with an invisible laser beam. But the room was packed, the cameras were rolling, and America was watching. Only Clinton knows if his approach was a conscious, at-the-moment decision or an automatic, subconscious approach based on years of refining his connection skills, knowing exactly what to do under what set of circumstances. The approach that night was probably the latter. After all, "practice makes perfect," and Clinton's approach was perfect.

Now view: www.youtube.com/watch?v=7ffbFvKlWqE

Sean Stephenson, one of Clinton's aides during his presidency, recognized and dissected Clinton's ability to connect. "Love him or loathe him, you can't deny that Bill Clinton is a masterful connection artist. I've seen him in action many times, and he's a wonder to behold. How does he do it? These were the techniques I saw him use most often:

1. He told a story.
2. He made physical contact.
3. He remembered your name.
4. He called you by name.
5. He made deep eye contact with you.
6. He used his facial expressions to convey his emotional state.
7. He calibrated his vocal inflections and volume based on the amount of rapport he had established.
8. He asked for your opinion.
9. He chose his words wisely.
10. He praised you publicly any chance he got."[3]

What Is a Connection?

A *connection* is the intangible but undeniable emotional or intellectual bond between people. Rick Pitino uses a metaphorical physical image, stating, "As a leader, what you're trying to do is *build bridges*."[4]

Certain enabling behaviors promote connection (or bridge building), which enhances other human-based behaviors such as communication, collaboration, respect, understanding, commitment, loyalty, and creativity. These, in turn, augment interpersonal relationships, creating an environment more conducive to driving change. John Maxwell links "connecting" with driving change: "*Connecting* is having the ability to identify with and relate to people in such a way that it increases your influence with them."[5] And influence drives change.

Four of these enabling behaviors will be discussed: Two come right from Clinton's playbook as described by Sean Stephenson.[6]

1. "He remembered your name." "He called you by name."

Our names are highly personal. They are central parts of our identities. Some claim that our names are the most important words to us.[7] Former Connecticut senator Chris Dodd claims that everybody's two favorite words are their first and last names.[8]

Remembering a name and calling someone by name are powerful displays of respect. The implication is you are important. You have enough value, integrity, and importance for me to remember your name. There is a jolt of pleasure for the recipient that touches the ego. The opposite of respect is disrespect, disregard, and contempt, so the omission of a name imparts a negative set of messages, often unintentionally.

Names are equalizers. The simple exchange, "Good morning, Sally." "Good morning, David," is powerful. Because names rarely have connotations, the two players are equal, regardless of positions or statuses, wealth, or education. The exchange is egalitarian. The uninformed observer does not know who the boss is and who the employee is, who is rich and who is poor, who is educated and who is not.

Greeting a person with his/her name opens doors to connecting at more personal and intimate levels as witnessed in the following anecdote: Greeting by name is "one way that the Old Corner Grocers used to keep their customers: 'Hello, Mrs. Pierce. How is your daughter doing, now that she's home from school?' The grocer is aiming at keeping Mrs. Pierce coming back to him for a lifetime."[9]

Remembering and calling someone by name can be learned. This ability is not innate. Although the practice may not imbue charisma, it enhances likeability and appeal. Literature contains methods and mnemonics for remembering names—two are cited—face association and repetition.[10]

2. "He made deep eye contact with you."

Eye contact has two definitions. One definition merely describes the connection when two people link eyesight. So, in its basic, most straightforward sense, eye contact is a noncontact, pseudo-physical connection. Similar to remembering and calling someone by his/her name, eye contact sends a powerful affirmation message to the partner.[11]

And again, any act that affirms connects. Eyes answer the critical ego-affirming questions for each participant: Is he/she paying attention to what I'm saying? Does this person find me attractive? Does this person like me?"[12]

The second definition recognizes the psychological and emotional messages and feelings that are conveyed via the eyes and their movements. *Eye contact:* "A meeting of the eyes between two people that expresses meaningful nonverbal communication."[13] Eye contact can express love, anger, approval, calmness, fear, anticipation, confusion, courage, faith, sincerity, doubt, and more. Also, according to Ramon Aldag and Buck Joseph, "Eye contact regulates conversations. Open-eye contact suggests understanding, interest, and inclusion. Seeking eye contact communicates one's desire to converse; avoiding eye contact conveys the opposite."[14]

Eye contact is probably the most intimate nonverbal, non-touching body sign between human beings. It is at the cusp of professionalism and sensuality, depending upon the situation and the intent. A traditional proverb states that the eyes are the window to the soul, implying an instantaneous, deep insight into the essence of the partner and his/her emotions.

Eye contact plays a vital but seldom-mentioned role in sports. On the field or court, it is a key way team players connect: the quarterback and the receiver, the shortstop and the first baseman, two volleyball players setting up a play. Eye contact speaks volumes: *Are you there? Are you ready? Can I count on you?* Author Zach Weismann's succinct quote mentions both eye contact and articulating his teammate's name: "We made eye contact. And I yelled to him. I yelled his name. I wanted the ball."[15]

The street peddler combing the intersection for contributions relies solely on eye contact to make his plea and on the driver's eyes to gauge the answer. The breastfeeding baby gazes directly into the mother's eyes, and they bond. The emotions exchanged during a slow dance ride back-and-forth on eye contact. Note that some cultures interpret eye contact differently from what is presented.

3. Listening

The topic of listening, similar to leadership, is complex and varied with the accompanying research, seminars, books, and Web sites. One Web site lists more than twenty-five types of listening, including active, casual, critical, false, judgmental, and therapeutic.[16]

The link between listening and connecting is related to respect and understanding. Regarding respect, listening conveys the same respect messages for the partner as eye contact. Regarding understanding, the connecting power of listening is summarized in Stephen Covey's habit 5: "Seek first to understand, then to be understood."[17] Wikipedia's summary captures the essence: Habit 5 uses "empathetic listening to be genuinely influenced by a person, which compels him/her to reciprocate the listening and take an open mind to being influenced by you. This creates an atmosphere of caring, respect, and positive problem solving."[18]

The first step to better listening, although a bit harsh and condescending and certainly not as sophisticated as Covey's advice, is to stop talking. Listening and talking simultaneously is a multitasking challenge that few can accomplish.

Linda Eve Diamond's "10 Rules of Listening"[19] is a constructive review, especially rule #6, which stresses "focus." She advises:

- **Give nonverbal clues.** Nod, lean toward the speaker, take on the general demeanor of someone who is interested.

- **Encourage the speaker to go on.** Especially over the phone, hearing no response feels like no one is listening.
- **Don't be a verbal trespasser.** A verbal trespasser is one who interrupts or finishes the speaker's sentences.
- **Ask open questions.** Open questions encourage the speaker. They elicit a more detailed response than closed questions. *What* and *why* are usually helpful starts to open questions.

Diamond reminds us to perform a "perception check." She states, "Summarizing is often helpful, especially if you have had a misunderstanding, are unsure of expectations, or have just reached an agreement. Ensure that everyone is coming away with the same idea."[20]

Diamond's rule #6 also contains a directive to "maintain eye contact," and rule #8 is, "Remember names." [21]

Finally, mastering the art of listening provides the opportunity to distinguish oneself from the masses. Francine Prose, author of *Reading Like a Writer: A Guide for People Who Love Books and for Those Who Want to Write Them,* states, "In life, it's rare that we truly are able to listen and find someone who will listen to us." [22] Who would not want to be that rare person?

4. Caring

A dictionary definition of caring is, "Feeling and exhibiting concern and empathy for others." Similar to involvement, caring has a dual imperative. First is the ethical imperative. It is the right thing to do. Second, it promotes connection and all the downstream benefits. Ralph Waldo Emerson said, "Trust men, and they will be true to you; treat them greatly, and they will show themselves great."[23]

Each leader must develop and refine his/her caring style. One astonishing set of caring guideposts is presented in www.goodcharacter.com and promoted in a video, *The Six Pillars of Character*, featuring the Popcorn Park Puppets.®[24] Although the set of guideposts is presented as a teaching guide on "Caring/Compassion" for grades Kindergarten through five, each of the guideposts also applies to the professional environment.

How to Be a Caring Person
- Treat people with kindness and generosity.
- Help people in need.
- Be sensitive to people's feelings.
- Never be mean or hurtful.
- Think about how your actions will affect others.
- Always remember, we become caring people by doing caring things!

Copyright Elkind+Sweet Communications / Live Wire Media.
Reprinted by permission. Copied from www.GoodCharacter.com.

Guidepost six: "We become caring people by doing caring things!" emphasizes the importance of a familiar theme, the "propensity to act." Similar to the change triad, in which steps one and two (vision and confidence) are useless without the action step three, in the caring twosome of feeling and exhibiting, feeling accomplishes little without exhibiting.

Recognizing the importance of what we say and what we do, the ultimate import is how the verbal and tangible affect how people feel. Maya Angelou elegantly states, "I've learned that people will forget what you said, people will forget what you did, but people will never forget how you made them feel."[25]

Some Final Thoughts
Revisiting Patrick Lencioni's three signs of a miserable job, connection combats anonymity and irrelevance.[26] If my boss or colleague knows my name, recalls my name, provides eye contact, listens to me, even touches me when appropriate, and commits acts of caring and concern, then I am not anonymous, and I am not irrelevant.

CHAPTER 3

Gratitude

appreciation • thankfulness • support • admiration
approval • agreement • recognition

Gratitude combats anonymity, irrelevance, and immeasurableness.

In 1864, Massachusetts Governor John A. Andrew wrote to President Abraham Lincoln, asking him to write to Mrs. Lydia Bixby, a widow who lost five sons during the Civil War. Here is Lincoln's letter:[1]

Executive Mansion
Washington, November 21, 1864

Dear Madam,

I have been shown in the files of the War Department a statement of the Adjutant General of Massachusetts that you are the mother of five sons who have died gloriously on the field of battle. I feel how weak and fruitless must be any word of mine which should attempt to beguile you from the grief of a loss so overwhelming. But I cannot refrain from tendering you the consolation that may be found in the thanks of the Republic they died to save. I pray that our Heavenly Father may assuage the anguish of your bereavement and leave you only the cherished memory of the loved and lost and the solemn pride that must be yours to have laid so costly a sacrifice upon the altar of freedom.

Yours very sincerely and respectfully,

A. Lincoln

Gratitude is the intangible but undeniable display of thankfulness, appreciation, or approval. Usually the display recognizes a personal quality, an accomplishment, or a deed.

The essence of gratitude for the recipient is self-esteem. Gratitude derives its power from our basic human need to feel good about ourselves. Displays of thankfulness, appreciation, or approval fill that need because we feel good about ourselves when we know that others hold us in high regard. What appears to often be a superficial exchange could be deceivingly intense and powerful. According to Sam Walton, the founder of WalMart stores, "Appreciate everything your associates do for the business. Nothing else can quite substitute for a few well-chosen, well-timed, sincere words of praise. They're absolutely free and worth a fortune."[2]

But the benefits of displays of gratitude are not exclusively related to enhancing the recipient's feelings of worth and esteem. First, human interactions that fulfill a basic human psychological or physical need, such as displays of gratitude, tend to bond. Bonding promotes connection, which cements the leader/employee interpersonal relationship and allegiance, all of which create an environment more conducive to change. Bestowing compliments or gifts establishes palpable energy transmission between the two parties. At first, the recipient says to himself about the provider, *She likes me,* and he detects a jolt of self-esteem. Then, immediately following, the recipient silently whispers, *I like me,* translating the affirmation to oneself, which in turn produces *I like her*, because she initiated the exchange. The recipient then offers a reciprocating comment acknowledging the initial exchange, such as, "I appreciate your comment," or "I appreciate the recognition," or "I appreciate the award," which replicates the cycle in a less perceptible, more compact way.

Here is a sample of a note to high performers:

> Sally, hi! Congratulations on your excellent performance review.
>
> Beth and I appreciate your hard work, effort, and your contribution to the care of our patients and to our department's mission.
>
> We are glad that you are on our team!
>
> Sincerely,
> Marc

It is not unusual to receive a reply such as the one below:

> Marc,
>
> Thank you for your kind words and recognition.
>
> Sally

This results in two energizing cycles. According to Bil Keane, creator of the comic strip *Family Circus,* "A hug is like a boomerang—you get it back right away."[3]

Second, Deborah Norville, anchor of the syndicated *Inside Edition,* in her book, *The Thank You Power: Making the Science of Gratitude Work for You,* says that employees are "prone to perform better because they know they are valued within the organization."[4] The work environment is pleasing to them, and they are happier.

Third, Norville also cites, "Evidence that individuals who are consciously and constantly grateful to others are happier, healthier, and less materialistic themselves; also, they tend to perform at higher levels."[5] Booker T. Washington agrees: "If you want to lift yourself up, lift up someone else."[6]

Finally, the gesture or act of gratitude serves as a window into the character of the provider. According to Rabbi Schmuley Boteach, "Gratitude is what establishes our humanity."[7] Gratitude means that you have the capacity to recognize the goodness, that you have the ability to package the recognition, and that you have the confidence to deliver it.

Scholars study Lincoln's letter to Mrs. Bixby not necessarily to determine the impact on her but what the letter reveals about Lincoln. What does the act of writing the letter and its contents reveal about a man who, after three harrowing years of war, surrounded by impatience and hate, carrying the guilt of the wreckage, with the outcome still undetermined, acknowledges a fellow politician by expressing the "thanks of the Republic" to a grieving widow? How many of us at the end of our normal workday rationalize not sending an e-mail to an employee who satisfied a customer, to a student who delivered a noteworthy presentation, or to a salesperson who captured a new client?

In 135 words, Lincoln displays the qualities and emotions that personify his magnificent aura: his ability to be factual, humble, empathetic, sensitive, grateful, spiritual, comforting, and patriotic, wrapped in caring, simplicity, and eloquence.

Dear Madam,

I have been shown in the files of the War Department a statement of the Adjutant General of Massachusetts that you are the mother of five sons who have died gloriously on the field of battle *(factual)*. I feel how weak and fruitless must be any word of mine *(humility)* which should attempt to beguile you *(empathy)* from the grief of a loss so overwhelming *(sensitivity)*. But I cannot refrain from tendering you the consolation that may be found in the thanks of the Republic they died to save *(gratefulness)*. I pray that our Heavenly Father may assuage the anguish of your bereavement *(spiritually)*, and leave you only the cherished memory of the loved and lost *(comforting)*, and the solemn pride that must be yours to have laid so costly a sacrifice upon the altar of freedom *(patriotic)*.

Yours very sincerely and respectfully,

A. Lincoln

Recognizing that a culture of gratitude might improve overall performance, enhance productivity of the leader and of the leader's unit, provide insights into the leader's character, and promote change, "real gratitude is an others-focused emotion in which the emphasis is on the giver," not for the betterment of the leader nor the improvement of the unit.[8] The benefits should be viewed as by-products, not goals of the exchanges.

Although gratitude is usually discussed as a display from a boss to an employee, a coach to a player, a president to a citizen, gratitude is not a one-way street. The appropriateness and value should be defined by the circumstances, the sincerity, and the delivery rather than the direction. This premise sets the stage for the employee to be the provider.

In the workplace, displaying gratitude to the boss gives the employee a platform to exhibit his/her character, confidence, and insight. An enlightened boss appreciates the qualities of the employee that the act represents. Many employees are reluctant to praise the boss for fear of being accused of having an ulterior motive— "buttering-up" the boss. But a wise employee renders those allegations petty compared with the need to recognize another human, even if the other human is the boss. When I have been praised, albeit occasionally, I have never imagined any motive other than the pure one.

A contrasting mode of gratitude is one without a mortal recipient. This behavior exhibits gratitude, not necessarily to others but rather for what one has. The manifestation is usually a silent, lone expression for one's own situation, condition, blessings, opportunities, friends, and family. According to author and counselor, Cherie Carter-Scott, "What really matters is to create a space in your consciousness for appreciation for all that you have now, so that you may live more joyously in your present moment."[9] Doing so creates an inner peace and humility that others detect, which projects confidence, calm, and authenticity, and that in turn contributes to a leadership aura.

Some Final Thoughts

Displays of gratitude have an addicting quality. All of us strive to duplicate the deeds or enhance our overall performances to get another "fix," the "psychic income." Recognizing the cause-and-effect phenomenon, Tom Peters teaches us to "celebrate what you want to see more of."[10]

A protocol (script) for verbal gratitude is helpful. Heidi Wall, the cofounder of the Flash Forward Institute, describes three steps:

1. Thank the person for something specific that he or she did for you. (It can also be something the person refrained from doing that would have hurt you.)
2. Acknowledge the effort it took for the person to help you by saying something like: "I know you didn't have to do _____," or "I know you went out of your way to do_____."
3. Tell the person the difference that his or her act personally made to you.[11]

Most experts agree that acknowledgments are most effective in affecting employee attitude and performance if the acknowledgments are "voluntary, detailed, immediate, and positive."[12] Contrast "Thanks for helping me calm the angry customer who just left," versus "Thanks for helping me with that customer," versus "I appreciate your help today." Some experts believe that constant displays of gratitude dilute the impact of the most deserving displays, but the numbers are not as important as the sincerity, content, and timeliness.

Public displays of gratitude have the added benefit of reinforcing the culture. Marcus Buckingham affirms, "When you bring an employee up onstage and praise her performance, this has a management impact. It will make this particular employee feel appreciated . . . . However, it will also, if you do it well, have a leadership impact. You are pointing to her and telling us that, although she is not perfect, her specific behaviors are the building blocks of our better future."[13]

Books are dedicated to outlining approaches to writing and delivering "thank-you" notes. Four are cited. [14, 15, 16, 17]

Revisiting Patrick Lencioni, gratitude-related techniques, practices, and behaviors combat anonymity and irrelevance. [18] If my boss or colleague recognizes me, my performance, or my contributions, then I am neither anonymous nor irrelevant. Also, if the gratitude is supported quantitatively by naming the person who sold the most appliances, scored the most runs, or received the most positive customer comments, then the displays of gratitude also combat immeasurableness.

In summary, one of the main messages in this chapter is to convey the power of gratitude—to expand the reader's paradigm to think of gratitude as not only a simple, meaningful exchange but also as a textured, potent, and significant element of leadership.

"To speak gratitude is courteous and pleasant, to enact gratitude is generous and noble, but to live gratitude is to touch Heaven." — Johannes Gaertner [19]

LEADERSHIP

CHAPTER 4

Responsiveness

awareness • sensitivity • alertness • confidence • reactiveness
accessibility • being interested

Responsiveness combats anonymity and irrelevance.

The name Maurice (Mo) Cheeks is not a household term, but avid basketball fans recognize the name. Mo Cheeks was born in 1956 in Chicago, Illinois, played basketball for West Texas State University, and was drafted by the Philadelphia 76ers in 1978. Cheeks played in the National Basketball Association (NBA) for fifteen years, eleven years for the 76ers. After his playing career, he started coaching.[1] A fair-minded assessment is that he was a near-great player, a good coach, and a superb humanitarian.

No description of the event that transpired on April 27, 2003, matches the one by journalist Robert J. Elisberg, published six years after the event. The following is truncated and paraphrased for conciseness. At the time of the event, Mo Cheeks served as coach of the NBA Portland Trailblazers.

"Today is the sixth anniversary of Maurice Cheeks' moment on the pedestal. For sheer emotional joy, it's hard to top what happened on April 27, 2003, before Game 4 of the NBA playoffs. The Portland Trailblazers and Dallas Mavericks prepared for their playoff game to start. Stepping out onto the court was Natalie Gilbert, a 13-year-old girl. Just another national anthem, just another youngster who won a contest, just another two minutes the crowd wanted to get past for the game they were there to see. And she started fine. Except that a few lines in, the high pageantry of the moment got her, and something went very wrong. She totally forgot the words. A young 13-year old child, standing in front of over 10,000 people, lost. Alone. And that's when Maurice Cheeks showed the kind of person he was."[2]

Just at the moment of high-anxiety and despair, Mo Cheeks sweeps into the scene, places his left hand reassuringly on Natalie's shoulder and starts singing. It doesn't take Natalie long to recapture her poise and her stride. Then Cheeks makes a series of decisions that embodies the nature of responsiveness. He gently lifts the microphone twice to Natalie's mouth, reestablishing a sense of normality and silently messaging, *This is yours to do. You can do it. Carry on.* Once she starts to roll again, he does not leave, probably for fear of a repeat. Natalie froze once; Cheeks wasn't going to allow it to happen again. Cheeks keeps his hand on Natalie's shoulder as a constant reminder that he is there, supporting her physically and emotionally, delicately balancing the need to be there for her versus the hazard of detracting from her spotlight. Then, he signals to the crowd to join in, establishing a sense of community. Cheeks simultaneously displays confidence and humility by unashamedly singing off-key, knowing that under the circumstances, his tonality did not matter.

Now view: http://www.youtube.com/watch?v=Em9wR9e5emY.

Exhibiting what is now known as a "Mo Cheeks' moment," he demonstrated the essence of his character and his leadership. Well, what change did he drive? First, he dramatically changed the course of that event. Plus, he changed the course of Natalie's life. When interviewed on *Good Morning, America*, she proudly announced that the "worst moment of her life" turned into "the best moment of my life."[3]

At the Trailblazers/Mavericks game, it is likely that all present were aware of Natalie's gaffe. It is also likely that all had the feelings of discomfort and empathy. So why was Mo Cheeks the first of the ten thousand people in the arena to respond? It's unlikely that a statistical anomaly produced Cheeks—that his "number was drawn." It is more likely that Mo Cheeks not only deeply understood the nature of leadership, but he also understood that his role demanded a heightened level of awareness, poise, and dynamism—more than just being the court admiral. Mo Cheeks executed the non-coaching leadership dimensions of his job that day. He rose to the occasion. He followed the three-step change model. He had a vision (to help Natalie), he had absolute confidence in that goal and in his ability to manage the situation, and he acted on it.

Mo Cheeks was the Coach of the Portland Trailblazers with an uppercase C and an uppercase M and L. The challenge is for lowercase managers and leaders to recognize, accept, and execute the leadership possibilities, per Lily Tomlin and Mother Teresa. Nothing dictated that only Mo Cheeks could act that day.

Cheeks also met Woodrow Wilson's challenge. Mo Cheeks was not on the court that day "merely to make a living." He allowed the spectators, players, coaches, and especially Natalie to "live more amply," and he did not "impoverish himself." In fact, Cheeks was demonstrative in celebrating his self-fulfillment. He allowed himself one luxurious moment of self-adulation, pumping his fist joyfully as he returned to his coaching station. "I was brought up the right way by my mother and my father," Cheeks said. "We didn't have the best life. But they instilled in us to treat people the right way. That's all that is. It's no secret. There's no recipe to it. It's just treating people correctly, and if you do it correctly, it'll come back to you."[4]

By doing the right thing, Mo Cheeks launched himself into the annals of humanitarian history. Of the top six Google® Mo Cheeks entries, four pertain to that moment. The first is a biographical Wikipedia® entry, which mentions the event, and the third one reviews his pro basketball statistics. The fourth entry, worth reading, is Randy Leonard's heartfelt description of the event. Leonard pays tribute: "Mo Cheeks, in a moment that epitomizes grace, presence of mind, kindness, and chivalry rescued one of these multi-conflicted, 13-year-old girls from potentially one of the most humiliating experiences of her young life."[5]

Bindu Sridhar presents a useful and perceptive definition of a "responsive leader." He writes, "A responsive leader is a person who is able to identify both the explicit and implicit needs of people . . . and uses his understanding of those needs to try and fulfill them, whenever required."[6] First, Sridhar recognizes "explicit" needs—the ones colleagues express: requests, suggestions, or desires. But Sridhar acknowledges that some needs are "implicit," not expressed. Natalie Gilbert's need was implicit. The complete leader has an acute awareness of both sets of needs and responds to both appropriately.

The complete leader is also acutely aware of the dynamics of the situation and the recipient's feelings. In this sense, the art of "responding" overlaps the art of "helping." In Edgar Schein's book *Helping: How to Offer, Give, and Receive Help*, he recommends that responders (Schein uses the word "helpers") "enter the dynamic in a supportive, giving, ego-enhancing way."[7] All of Mo Cheeks' verbal and nonverbal cues and actions were just that, avoiding the emergence of feelings of belittlement, embarrassment, or lack of ability on Natalie's part. She was drowning, and Cheeks responded in a manner that preserved her esteem. The final warm, accepting, and complete hug "sealed the deal."

A dictionary definition of *responsiveness* is "responding with emotion to people and events." The phrase, "responding with emotion," erases the sense of obligatory duty and instead imparts energy, joy, and sincerity that transform the science of leadership into an art form—one that inspires, empowers, and unites. Mo Cheeks did all. He was completely wrapped into the moment—its needs and opportunities. Every one of his movements—his facial expressions, his eye movements, his hand gestures—epitomized a man completely involved in his mission.

Responding instantaneously to either implicit or explicit needs may not always be critical. In some situations, "Getting back to you next week" will suffice, as will placing an unrequested water cooler in a work area several weeks after recognizing a need. However, in other situations, fractions of seconds may differentiate between success and failure. Lifeguards and firefighters know that. Recognizing the frequent importance of reaction time, a dictionary's second definition of *responsive* is "quick to react or respond appropriately." Mo Cheeks did not have the luxury of pondering. His "propensity to act" instantly converted into acting. Thomas Jefferson shouts, "Act! Action will delineate and define you."[8] As we have seen, action delineated and defined Mo Cheeks.

Youtube® appropriately entitles the Natalie Gilbert/Mo Cheeks video, *Leadership and Attitude at the Right Time.*

Some Final Thoughts

A precursor to responsiveness is awareness. Unless one is responding to an expressed need, one must first be aware of a disparity between what is and what could be. The sense of disparity provokes a sense of discontent and then opportunity. According to Cherie Carter-Scott, "Paying attention to your feelings is the easiest way to get in touch with your inner machinations. Feelings are the lights on the dashboard of life; when one is illuminated, you can be sure it is a signal of some . . . issue that needs to be addressed."[9]

The feelings create the need to form a view of what could be—the future, the vision. After the vision is formed, confidence propels the propensity to act. If one is unaware, or if the awareness doesn't provoke feelings, then the cascade stops. One is robbed of the difficulties, agonies, challenges, and ultimately, the pleasures, growth, and rewards, even the ecstasy of the accomplishment or the victory. The passengers of United 93 on 9/11 are heralded as heroes because of their awareness, their astuteness, and their courage in devising and executing a plan to avoid a likely but unconfirmed disaster. They knew they were sacrificing their lives, only suspecting that their efforts would save countless others.

The sibling of responsiveness is decisiveness. Except in the circumstances that permit a time frame, responsiveness mandates quick decisions. Mo Cheeks made such decisions: when to enter, how to stand, when to smile, when to touch, when to exit, when to self-adulate. Decisiveness strikes at the heart of what followers want from their leaders, often comprising strength, courage, intelligence, spirit—all in the name of making meaningful change for the good of the "order," whether the order be the family, the club, the team, the department, the company, the teenager, or the nation. Political commentator James Carville admonished President Obama's indecisiveness regarding the oil-spill cleanup. "This president needs to tell BP, 'I'm in charge. You're going to do what we say.'"[10]

An appreciation of the value of leadership qualities can be achieved not only by studying cases like Clinton's, Lincoln's, and Cheeks,' which represent the finest exhibitions, but also by studying cases that exemplify leadership voids. One can illustrate the positive by revealing the negative. In the decade of the 2000s, both presidents of the United States, as the leaders ultimately responsible for federal government mobilization and effectiveness, were slow to respond to major domestic crises and were justifiably criticized. George W. Bush's inability to recognize the extent of the Katrina disaster and to rally the rescue operations caused immeasurable economic harm and human suffering—a blunder that Barack Obama inexcusably repeated after the BP oil spill but to a lesser extent.[11, 12, 13] Although a lack of leadership is often viewed as an endorsement of the status quo and merely a missed opportunity for positive change, leadership vacuums can create damage.

Revisiting Patrick Lencioni, responsiveness combats two of the three signs of a miserable job.[14] If my boss or colleague recognizes my need, either expressed or not, I am neither anonymous nor irrelevant.

Epilogue

Some say that at its core, leadership is about vision. Others claim it's about personality and charisma, influence and persuasion, relationships and friendships, equity and service, or truth and integrity. I make an argument for change.

Regardless of the core composition, leadership is about all of those things and more. Many elements are connected, intertwined, or are inseparable. They can be circular; a cause that produces an effect can result in the effect promoting the cause. For example, relationships can lead to successful change, and the resulting achievement can cement relationships. Also, as Thomas Carlyle claims, "Nothing builds self-esteem and self-confidence like accomplishment,"[1] and self-esteem and self-confidence fuel accomplishment.

Regarding the number and selection of elements composing employee-centered leadership (connection, gratitude, responsiveness), there is value in simplicity. In the movie *Bull Durham*, Kevin Costner plays an over-the-hill, minor league catcher and mentor, Crash Davis. Davis tells rookie Calvin LaLoosh, played by Tim Robbins, "This is a very simple game. You throw the ball, you catch the ball, you hit the ball."[2] Well, we know that baseball is not a simple game; it's excruciatingly complex. But executing those three acts well has solitary value and provides a basis for building knowledge and skills.

If the proposed approach to employee-centered leadership can stand alone, has integrity and truth, and provides a foundation to build upon, it has value. As a leader, drive meaningful change. Recognize that meaningful change is more likely accomplished with involved, enthusiastic, and empowered employees. Believe that connecting with employees, appreciating them, and responding to their explicit and implicit needs promotes those desired qualities.

Tonya, the boss and chair of the regular Monday morning staff meeting, met Warren, a fellow staff member, at the coffee bar before the meeting. She made deep eye contact with him and smiled.

"Warren, good morning. How are you? May I get you a cup—cream, no sugar, I believe? I see your Steelers crushed my Ravens yesterday." And off they went to the meeting. On their way down the hall, she said, "Warren, thanks for getting the report to me on Friday. Good job. I made only two changes."

Notes

Introduction

[1] James M. Kouzes and Barry Z. Posner, The Truth About Leadership: The No-Fads, Heart-of-the-Matter Facts You Need to Know (San Francisco: Jossey-Bass, 2010).

[2] Stephen Covey, The Seven Habits of Highly Effective People, rev. ed. (New York: Free Press, 2004).

Chapter 1: The Essence and Nature of Leadership

[1] David McCullough, The Great Bridge: The Epic Story of the Building of the Brooklyn Bridge (New York: Simon and Schuster, 2001).

[2] Wikipedia, "The Brooklyn Bridge," en.wikipedia.org/wiki/Brooklyn Bridge.

[3] Marie Kane, "Leadership: Today's Requirements and Tomorrow's Challenges," Executive Evolution: Creating Superb Organizations, 2004. (Portions originally published in Competitive Edge magazine.) http://www.leader-values.com/article.php?aid+290.

[4] C. F. Rauch and O. Behling, "Functionalism: The Basis for an Alternate Approach to the Study of Leadership," in J. G. Hunt, D. M. Hosking, C. A. Schriesheim, and R. Stewart, eds. Leaders and Managers: International Perspectives on Managerial Behaviour and Leadership Research (Elmsford, New York: Pergamon Press, 1984), 45–50.

[5] Garry Wills, Certain Trumpets: The Nature of Leadership (New York: Simon and Schuster, 1995).

[6] Marcus Buckingham, The One Thing You Need to Know: About Great Managing, Great Leading, and Sustained Individual Success (New York: Free Press, 2005).

[7] John P. Kotter, "What Leaders Really Do," Harvard Business Review 68 (May–June 1990): 103–111.

[8] Peter Northouse, Leadership: Theory and Practice, 5th ed. (Los Angeles: Sage, 2010).

[9] Ken Blanchard, Brainy Quotes, "Ken Blanchard Quotes," http://www.brainyquote,com/quotes/authors/k/ken_blanchard.html.

[10] Ken Blanchard, The Heart of a Leader: Insights on the Art of Influence (Colorado Springs, CO: David C. Cook, 2007).

[11] Jeffrey Immelt in E. Hwang, "Managing Organizations in the 'Projectized' Way," http://baj-conference.org/BAI2011/Papers/8.Others8362.pdf.

[12] Rick Pitino, Lead to Succeed: 10 Traits of Great Leadership in Business and Life (New York: Broadway Books, 2001).

[13] John C. Maxwell, *The 21 Indispensable Qualities of a Leader: Becoming a Person Others Will Want to Follow* (Nashville: Thomas Nelson, 2007).

[14] Peter F. Drucker, *The Best of Sixty Years of Peter S. Drucker's Essential Writings on Management* (New York: Harper Business, 2008).

[15] Martin Luther King Jr., "I Have a Dream," August 28, 1963, www.mtholyoke.edu/acad/intrel/speech/dream.htm.

[16] Pitino, *Lead to Succeed.*

[17] Mother Teresa, *Quotations Book,* http://quotationsbook.com/quote/668.

[18] Lily Tomlin, *Thinkexist.com,* "Lily Tomlin Quotes," http://thinkexist.com/quotation/i-always-wondered-why-somebody-doesn-t-do/361406.html.

[19] John P. Kotter, *John P. Kotter on What Leaders Really Do* (Boston: Harvard Business School Press, 1999).

[20] Jim Calhoun, *A Passion to Lead: Seven Leadership Secrets for Success in Business, Sports, and Life* (New York: St. Martin's Griffin, 2008).

[21] Tom Peters, *Brainy Quotes,* "Tom Peters Quotes," http://www.brainyquote.com/quotes/quotes/t/tompeters166169.html.

[22] Warren Bennis, "University of Maryland Symposium" (1988), in Louis D. Eigen and Jonathan P. Siegel, *The Manager's Book of Quotations* (Rockville, MD: AMACOM, 1991).

[23] Theodore Hesburgh, *Thinkexist.com,* Theodore Hesburgh Quotes," http://thinkexist.com/quotes/theodore_hesburgh/.

[24] "What Is Existentialism?" http://media.wiley.com/product_data/excerpt/91/04702769/0470276991.pdf.

[25] Peter N. Zarlenga, *Thinkexist.com,* "Peter Nivio Zarlenga Quotes," http://thinkexist.com/quotes/peter_nivio_zarlenga/.

[26] Oprah Winfrey, http://www.values.com/inspirational-quotes/6395-create-the-highest-grandest.

[27] Mike Vance and Diane Deacon, *Think Out of the Box* (Franklin Lakes, NJ: Career Press, 1997).

[28] Shel Silverstein, Thinkexist.com, "Shel Silverstein Quotes," http://thinkexist.com/quotation/listen_to_the_mustn-ts-child-listen_to_the_don-ts/151628.html.

[29] Antoine de Saint-Exupery, *Flight to Arras* (India: Thomson Press, 2008).

[30] Stuart R. Levine, *The Six Fundamentals of Success: The Rules for Getting It Right for Yourself and Your Organization* (New York: Crown Business, 2006).

[31] Cicero, in J. K. Hoyt, ed., *Cyclopedia of Practical Quotations* (New York: Funk and Wagnalls, 1907).

[32] Jesse Jackson, *Thinkexist.com*, "Jesse Jackson Quotes," http://thinkexist.com/quotation/if-my-mind-can-conceive-it-and-my-heart-can/362008.html.

[33] Harry S. Truman, *Goodreads*, http:www.goodreads.com/author/quotes/203941.Harry_S_Truman.

[34] Catherine Pulsifer, *Inspirational Quotes*, "Catherine Pulsifer Quotes," http://www.inspirationalquotes4u.com/pulsiferquotes/index.html.

[35] Pablo Picasso, *Thinkexist.com*, "Pablo Picasso Quotes," http://thinkexist.com/quotation/action_is_the_foundational_key_to_all_success/218333.html.

[36] David Mahoney in B. Moawad, *Whatever It Takes* (Seattle: WA: Compendium, 1995).

[37] John Wanamaker in T. Connor, *81 Challenges Smart Managers Face* (Naperville, IL: Sourcebooks, 2007).

[38] Samuel Johnson, *Brainy Quotes*, "Samuel Johnson Quotes," http://brainyquote.com/quotes/quotes/s/samueljohn122057.html

[39] Arnold Schopenhauer, *SBSA Partners, LLC*, "Sustainability," http://sbsapartners.com/ideas/sustainabilityquotes.php.

[40] Cardinal J. H. Newman, *Thinkexist.com*, http://thinkexist.com/quotation/a_man_would_do_nothing_if_he_waited_until_he/210254.html.

[41] Roslyn Carter, *The Quotations Page*, http://www.quotationspage.com/quote/2415.html.

[42] John P. Kotter, *Leading Change* (Boston: Harvard Business School Press, 1996).

[43] "Soup King Nourishes an Ailing Hometown," *Executive Leadership* 27 (Feb. 2012): 2.

[44] Vance and Deacon, *Think Out of the Box*.

[45] Indira Gandhi in Bob Phillips, *Book of Great Thoughts and Funny Sayings* (Wheaton, IL: Tyndale, 1993).

[46] R. L. Katz, "Skills of an Effective Administrator," *Harvard Business Review* 33 (Jan.–Feb. 1955): 33–42.

[47] Laurence J. Peter and Raymond Hull, *The Peter Principle* (Cutchogue, NY: Buccaneer Books, 1996).

[48] W. J. King and James G. Skakoon, *The Unwritten Laws of Business* (New York: Doubleday, 2007).

[49] L. C. Spears, "Practicing Servant Leadership," *Leader to Leader* 34 (Fall 2004): 7–11.

[50] J. W. Sipe and D. M. Frick, Seven Pillars of Servant Leadership: Practicing the Wisdom of Leading by Serving (Mahwah NJ: Paulist Press, 2009).

[51] Charlene Li, *Open Leadership: How Social Technology Can Transform the Way You Lead* (San Francisco: Jossey–Bass, 2010).

[52] Robert K. Greenleaf, *Servant Leadership: A Journey into the Nature of Legitimate Power and Greatness* (Mahwah, NJ: Paulist Press, 2002).

[53] Benjamin Christopher, *Why Didn't I Think of That?* "Google's Eight Rules for Being a Good Manager," http://thinkofthat.net/2011/03/21/googles-8-rules-for-being-a-good-manager/.

[54] T. H. Davenport and Harris J. Shapiro, "Competing on Talent Analytics," *Harvard Business Review* 88 (Oct. 2010): 52–58.

[55] Adam Bryant, *New York Times,* "Google's Quest to Build a Better Boss," http://www.nytimes.com/2011/03/13/business/13hire.html?pagewanted-all.

[56] N. Cowan, "The Magical Number 4 in Short-term Memory: A Reconsideration of Mental Storage Capacity," *Behavioral and Brain Sciences* 24 (2000): 87–183.

[57] Woodrow W. Wilson, *Brainy Quotes,* "Woodrow Wilson Quotes," http://www.brainyquote.com/quotes/quotes/w/woodrowwil121798.html.

[58] Patrick Lencioni, *The Three Signs of a Miserable Job: A Fable for Managers (and Their Employees)* (San Francisco: Jossey–Bass, 2007).

[59] Ibid.

[60] Mother Teresa, *Thinkexist.com,* "Mother Teresa Quotes," http://thinkexist.com/quotation/the_most_terrible_poverty_is_loneliness_and_the/216333.html.

[61] Lencioni, *Three Signs.*

[62] Katharine Graham, *Thinkexist.com,* "Katharine Graham Quotes," http://thinkexist.com/quotation/to_love_what_you_do_and_feel_that_it_matters_how/213126.html.

[63] Lencioni, *Three Signs.*

[64] David Novak, *Taking People with You: The Only Way to Make Big Things Happen* (New York: Portfolio/Penquin, 2012).

[65] Gary Yuki, *Leadership in Organizations,* 8th ed. (Englewood Cliffs, NJ: Prentice–Hall, 2012).

[66] Northouse, *Leadership.*

[67] Kane, "Leadership."

[68] John Gardner, *On Leadership* (New York: Free Press, 1993).

[69] Maxwell, *Indispensable Qualities.*

[70] John Zenger, Joseph Folkman, and Scott Ediger, "Making Yourself Indispensable," *Harvard Business Review* 89 (Oct. 1955): 85–92.

71 D. R. Hampton, *Management*, 3rd ed. (New York: McGraw-Hill, 1986).

72 Ulysses S. Grant, "Our White House: Looking In, Looking Out," http://www.ourwhitehouse.org/prespgs/usgrant.html.

Chapter 2: Connection

1 Newton M. Minow, Craig L. LaMay, and Vartan Gregorian, *Inside the Presidential Debates: Their Improbably Past and Promising Future* (Chicago: University of Chicago Press, 2008). Excerpt: "Memorable Moments from Presidential Debates." http://www.press.uchicago.edu/Misc/Chicago/530413.html.

2 Alex Markels, "George H. W. Bush Checks His Watch During Debate with Bill Clinton and Ross Perot," *U. S. News and World Report* (2008, Jan. 17). http://www.usnews.com/news/politics/articles/2008/01/17/a-damaging-impatience.

3 Sean Stephenson, *Get Off Your "But": How to End Self-Sabotage and Stand Up for Yourself* (San Francisco: Jossey–Bass, 2009). Excerpt: "10 Things I Learned about Connection from President Bill Clinton" in http://www.philgerbyshak.com/connection-from-president-bill-clinton.

4 Rick Pitino, *Lead to Succeed: 10 Traits of Great Leadership in Business and Life* (New York; Broadway Books, 2001).

5 John C. Maxwell, *The 5 Levels of Leadership: Proven Steps to Maximize Your Potential* (New York: Center Street, 2011).

6 Stephenson, *Get Off Your "But."*

7 B. Bennett, *Year to Success,* "Remembering and Using People's Names." http://www.yeartosuccess.com/YearToSuccess-sample.pdf.

8 Jim Calhoun, *A Passion to Lead: Seven Leadership Secrets for Success in Business, Spots, and Life* (New York: St. Martin's Griffin, 2008).

9 A. M. Hughes, "The Importance of Recognition," (Oct. 19, 2011). http://www.dbmarketing.com/articles/Art191.htm.

10 *Mind Tools*: "How to . . . Remember People's Names." http://www.mindtools.com/pages/article/newTIM_12.htm.

11 *AudioEnglish.net*. "Eye Contact." Definition. http://www.audioenglish.net/dictionary/eye_contact.htm.

12 V. Kotelnikov, "Connecting with People." http://www.1000ventures.com/business_guide/crosscuttings/people_connecting.html.

13 *AudioEnglish.net*, "Eye Contact."

14 Ramon Aldag and Buck Joseph, *Leadership and Vision: 25 Keys to Motivation* (New York: Lebhar–Friedman Books, 2000).

[15] Zach Weismann, *Thinkexist*, "Zach Weismann Quotes," http://thinkexist.com/quotation/we-made-eye-contact-and-i-yelled-to-him-i-yelled/1027070.html.

[16] *Changing Minds: Many Types of Listening*, http://changingminds.org/techniques/listening/all_types_listening_htm.

[17] Stephen Covey, *The Seven Habits of Highly Effective People*, rev. ed. (New York: Free Press, 2004).

[18] *Wikipedia*, "The Seven Habits of Highly Effective People," http://en.wikipedia.org/wiki/The_Seven_Habits_of_Highly_Effective_People .

[19] Linda Eve Diamond, *1000 Advices*, "10 Rules of Listening." http://www.1000advices.com/guru/listening_10rules_led.html.

[20] Ibid.

[21] Ibid.

[22] Francine Prose, Reading Like a Writer: A Guide for People Who Love Books and for Those Who Want to Write Them (New York: Harper Perennial, 2007).

[23] Ralph Waldo Emerson, *Brainy Quotes*, "Trust Quotations," http://www.brainyquote.com/quotes/keywords/trust.html.

[24] *Good Character.com*, "The Six Pillars of Character," "How to Be a Caring Person," http://www.goodcharacter.com/pp/caring.html.

[25] Maya Angelou in K. Browne, *101 Ways to Say Thank You* (New York: Sterling Publishing, 2008).

[26] Patrick Lencioni, *The Three Signs of a Miserable Job: A Fable for Managers (and Their Employees)* (San Francisco: Jossey–Bass, 2007).

Chapter 3: Gratitude

[1] Abraham Lincoln, "Letter to Mrs. Bixby." http://showcase.netins.net/web/creative/lincoln/speeches/bixby.htm.

[2] Sam Walton, *Thinkexist.com*, "Sam Walton Quotes," http://thinkexist.com/quotation/appreciate_everything_your_associates_do_for_the_149400.html.

[3] Bil Keane, *Thinkexist.com*, "Bil Keane Quotes." http://thinkexist.com/quotation/a_hug_is_like_a_boomergang-you_get_it_back_right/200279.html.

[4] Deborah Norville, Thank You Power: Making the Science of Gratitude Work for You (Nashville: Thomas Nelson, 2007).

[5] Ibid.

[6] Booker T. Washington, *Brainy Quotes*, "Booker T. Washington Quotes," http://brainyquote.com/quotes/authors/b/booker_t_washington.html.

[7] Schmuley Boteach, *Renewal: A Guide to the Values-Filled Life* (New York: Basic Books, 2010).

[8] Norville, *Thank You Power.*

[9] Cherie Carter-Scott, If Life Is a Game, These Are the Rules: Ten Rules for Being Human as Introduced in Chicken Soup for the Soul (New York: Crown Archetype, 1998).

[10] Tom Peters, *Thinkexist.com*, "Tom Peters Quotes," http://thinkexist.com/quotation/celebrate_what_to_see_more_of/264684.html.

[11] Heidi Wall in K. Ferrazzi, *When Thanks Isn't Enough: 3 Steps to Gratitude That Empowers.* http://www.keithferrazzi.com/communication.

[12] J. Trinka. *GovLeaders.org.* "What's a Manager to Do? http://govleaders.org/whats_a_manager_to_do.htm.

[13] Marcus Buckingham, The One Thing You Need to Know: About Great Managing, Great Leading, and Sustained Individual Success (New York: Free Press, 2005).

[14] J. Kralik, *A Simple Act of Gratitude: How Learning to Say Thank You Changed My Life* (New York: Hyperion, 2011).

[15] Robyn F. Spizman, The Thank You Book: Hundreds of Clever, Meaningful, and Purposeful Ways to Say Thank You (Kenneshaw, GA: Active Parenting, 2002).

[16] K. Browne, *101 Ways to Say Thank You* (New York: Sterling Publishing, 2008).

[17] Johannes Gaertner in K. Browne, *101 Ways to Say Thank You* (Sterling Publishing, 2008).

[18] Patrick Lencioni, *The Three Signs of a Miserable Job: A Fable for Managers (and Their Employees)* (San Francisco: Jossey-Bass, 2007).

[19] Gaertner in Browne, *101 Ways to Say Thank You.*

Chapter 4: Responsiveness

[1] *Wikipedia*, "Mo Cheeks," http://en.wikipedia.org/wiki/Maurice_Cheeks.

[2] Robert J. Elisberg, "Oh, Say Can You Sing? A National Anthem to Remember." *Huffington Post* (April 27, 2009). http://www.huffingtonpost.com/robert-j-elisberg/happy-maurice-cheeks-day_b_854304.html.

[3] *FunTimesGuide*. "Ohhh, Say Can You SING?" http://thefuntimeguide.com/2004/10/ohhh_say_can_you.php.

[4] D. Mayberry, "Star-Spangled Save: What Maurice Cheeks Did for Anthem Singer in Portland Is Still Remembered." In *NewsOK*. http://newsok.com/star-spangled-save-what-marice-cheeks-did-for-anthem-singer-in-portland-is-still-remembered/article/3413717.

[5] R. Leonard, "Mo Cheeks and Natalie Gilbert," *Blue Oregon* (March 3, 2005). http://www.blueoregon.com/2005/03/mo_cheeks_and_n/.

[6] B. Sridhar, "Leadership by Responsiveness," *The Hindu* (June 30, 2004).

[7] Edgar H. Schein, *Helping: How to Offer, Give, and Receive Help* (San Francisco: Berrett–Koehler Publishers, 2011).

[8] Thomas Jefferson, *Brainy Quotes*, "Action Quotes," http://www.brainyquote.com/quotes/keywords/action.html.

[9] Cherie Carter–Scott, If Life Is a Game, These Are the Rules: Ten Rules for Being Human as Introduced in Chicken Soup for the Soul (New York: MJF Books, 1998).

[10] James Carville, "Perspectives." *Newsweek* (June 7, 2010): 16.

[11] *Foreign Mail Service*, "Obama Too Slow to Act Against Oil Slick Disaster, Threatening Species Along the Coast." http:www.dailymail.co.uk/news/article-1270151/Obama-slow-act-oil-slick-disaster.html#ixzz1iLMZifgm.

[12] *Wikipedia*, "Criticism of government response to Hurricane Katrina," http://en.wikipedia.org/wiki/Criticism_of_government_response_to_Hurricane_Katrina.

[13] Ali Frick, "Bush On Katrina: 'Don't Tell Me The Federal Response Was Slow,'" *ThinkProgress.org* (2009 Jan 12). http://thinkprogress.org/politics/2009/01/12/34684/bush-defends-katrina-response/.

[14] Patrick Lencioni, *The Three Signs of a Miserable Job: A Fable for Managers (and Their Employees)* (San Francisco: Jossey–Bass, 2007).

Epilogue

[1] Thomas Carlyle in John C. Maxwell, *The 5 Levels of Leadership: Proven Steps to Maximize Your Potential* (New York: Center Street, 2011).

[2] *Bull Durham*, Orion Pictures, 1988.